68 Years to Closure

Robert Earl Cobb

Rober Earl Cobb
68 Years to Closure

All rights reserved
Copyright © 2024 by Robert Earl Cobb

No part of this publication may be reproduced, distributed, or transmitted in any form or by any means, including photocopying, recording, or other electronic or mechanical methods, without the prior written permission of the publisher, except in the case of brief quotations embodied in critical reviews and certain other noncommercial uses permitted by copyright law.

Published by Spines
ISBN: 979-8-89383-482-6

Dedication

Dedicated to my entire family,
past, present and, future.

Me and Dad about to hang out

Acknowledgment

Acknowledging my best friend and brother Willie R McGhee Bka Idris and family.

Me and Willie McGhee. Idris.

Table of Contents

About the Author

Throughout my entire life, I've been committed to doing the right thing. Acknowledging the most high has always been my priority. And knowing my roots has always been my ultimate goal in life.

My graduation picture
Canton McKinley H.S. class of 1973.

Chapter 1

In the vibrant city of Birmingham, Alabama, a remarkable soul entered the world on a fateful September 21st, 1953. This soul, which would soon be known as yours truly me, arrived with an enigmatic feature that stirred both wonder and bewilderment—a delicate veil or caul that veiled my face at birth. It was as if destiny had woven a layer of mystery into my very being, bestowing upon me an extraordinary gift that some deemed supernatural, yet I, at times, perceived as a perplexing curse.

My mother, Lilly Mae Cobb, was merely 14 years old when she brought me into this world, facing the challenging task of motherhood at a tender age. She wasn't ready to be a mom to a little boy when she was still a child. She had never envisioned herself nursing a child at such an early age. However, fate had different plans, and my grandparents, the resilient Square and Rhoda Cobb, courageously embraced the role of raising me. They stepped in like angels in my life and protected me from all the evil this world was surrounded with.

My entrance into the world was not without its challenges, as this unique caul had to be gently removed to grant me the gift of sight. Little did I know, this act would serve as a gateway to a realm beyond the ordinary—a realm of visions, déjà vu experiences, and an uncanny ability to perceive and communicate with the departed souls that lingered among us.

Life took an unexpected turn as my grandmother's emotions swirled like a tempest, prompting a move from the Southern charm of Birmingham to the distant landscapes of Ohio. Settling in the vibrant communities of Cleveland and Canton, we started a new chapter cloaked in family ties and connections. The motivation behind this move was more than mere geography; it was an important decision that concealed my existence from my father, John Edward Peoples. A man of 25 years back then, he unknowingly walked the same streets, unaware of the extraordinary life that had begun with his seed.

Driven by both curiosity and determination, I started a personal journey to uncover the hidden truths about my family history. My grandmother, fueled by anger, would sometimes talk about a man named Johnny Peoples, who had a light skin color, and oddly, this description matched my father when I finally found him. This curiosity led me to start searching for my father. He looked exactly as I had envisioned him. As though he had preserved himself so I would recognize him, when we met.

My mother seemed distant during my childhood, and my memories of her were unclear. I would not see her often, and my grandparents would make me call her by her nickname, Sister. For a very long time, I was unaware of the fact that she was the woman had who had given birth to me and brought my existence into this world. I only remembered her as a young girl who was always caught up in the responsibilities of life, including her studies. However, I, on the other hand, was someone who only always received love from everywhere. Despite being so busy with their work, my grandparents took care of me and raised me.

My sister and brother were both born in Cleveland, Ohio. Their father, a man named Stover, was a part of our lives, even though he wasn't always there. One special Christmas when I was three years old, my mother, her husband, and my siblings visited us in Canton. We shared hugs and warmth, enjoying the holiday season. This memory became important to me because it was one of the last times I saw my mother and siblings for a long while.

Things changed in 1960 when I was about seven years old. This year became important because it revealed something unexpected. My grandmother told me that my mother would be coming back home soon . This was surprising news to me, because I had thought my grandmother was my mother. These complex connections between family members that I didn't fully understand started to become clear. Therefore I was waiting eagerly for my mother's arrival. My grandmother, family, and friends gathered in the living room waiting for my mother's bus to come in from only God knows where.

My grandmother sent me upstairs to bed so the grown folk could talk. I stayed awake, like it were Christmas Eve. Eventually I creeped downstairs to the bathroom. In leaving the bathroom, I noticed a new comer in the living room. A very beautiful young lady in a red dress. My heart began to pound, my eyes began to water, I knew this was her. So I ran to her and leaped into her arms. Tears of joy over came the both of us. Little did I know this was the beginning of a my journey to closure. Starting with the first seven years of my life not knowing who I was.

Things weren't easy when my mother surfaced. She was very secretive about the several years she had disappeared, and the things that had taken place in her life. My birth certificate says my mom's birth name was Lillie, but she introduced herself as Felounese. I have no idea the conversations that took place with the family about this change of name. So everyone continued just addressing her by her nickname, Sister. Once Mom settled in, I began to ask questions about my father. She often blew me off by saying that negro was a cab driver in Birmingham, That's all I remember. But I continued to ask over the years.

Growing up with my mother was a mixture of love with difficulties due to her bad choices regarding her male companions. I even stood up against grown men during my teenage years to protect her. She had a tough image, but my love for her kept me grounded. My education of life had begun. At the age of fourteen, just like my mother, I had to take on the responsibility of becoming a man. I started working to provide my own school clothes, and at sixteen, I bought my first car.

Sports, especially football and track wrestling, became a big part of my youth. They helped shape my identity and created strong bonds through competition. I started out playing flag football, then I joined a separate league and a team called the Mohawks. This was my first time ever playing in uniform. I played football through high school, and beyond. I never became a big star athlete, but 1 loved the game. I learned the importance of teamwork. I did have dreams of playing in the NFL. I learned later that I was more drawn to entertainment, in which I pursued later.

The first 19 years of my life had been a testament to faith, anchored within the walls of our family church.

My grandmother had me in church at least six days a week. This instilled in me the value of faith, and bonding with children just like me. In all actuality these were the most fun times in my life. This introduced me to traveling going to church conventions and counsel meeting and making friends everywhere. Back then we did not have the means of communication that we have now so we got phone numbers and addresses from the new friends we were making. Our letter writing at that time was called pen pals.

Writing and sharing pictures was our way of communicating back then. When I was a senior in high school, I decided that college wasn't for me, so I joined the Air Force straight out of high school.

In 1973, I went to boot camp at Lackland Air Force Base in San Antonio, Texas. Upon completing my basic training, I went to Air Force security tech school, where I became an SP. This was a pretty good job, guarding aircraft and occasional doing base patrol duties. All went well until I got stationed on my first base at Altus Air Force Base in Altus Oklahoma. In a matter of months, my whole life turned around. After living in the security barracks on base, I decided to move off base. I moved into the trailer behind someone's house for a few months. Eventually, I met two fellow airmen, one from Detroit and the other from New York. The three of us decided to rent a three-bedroom trailer off-base. We all work different shifts, so we didn't see each other very much. One fateful day, my roommate from New York disappeared. A day later, my other roommate and I were taken to the sheriff's department for questioning about several robberies. After being questioned, we found that our roommate from New York was involved in the robberies along with several other individuals. After being questioned and released the other individuals were arrested on the base. The word was out that I was a snitch in which I wasn't because I didn't know any of these individuals. So I began to get death threats from their friends. Eventually I was put in a position to make a decision. Stay in the military or take a discharge so I took the discharge to protect my life. I was discharged in January of 1975.

Back on the streets where I grew up, I had to find a way to understand who I was all over again. I turned back to music in pursuit of my identity. I returned to the group that I performed with while I was on leave from the service. I picked up some new skills, learning a little bit about the bass guitar, but my favorite was percussion and, of course, my gift of being a vocalist, just like my father.

Actually, the band that I was with was fairly talented and probably could have gone places. Eventually I became the lead singer of the group. We were pretty popular locally throughout the Northwest area of Ohio. We actually had recording sessions at Red Top recording studio in Lorain Ohio. After one of our performances I was offered to leave the group and go solo. My father-in-law who was our manager encouraged me to make the move. But due to my loyalty to the group that had taken me in, I turned down the offer. After a few years, the group broke up, and I turned to be coming a DJ. And I still do that today.

The search for my dad was a continuous quest in my life. It was like working on a jigsaw puzzle that I refused to give up on. At this time of my life is one of the many times I reverted back to my search. For some reason, I never gave hope that my father was still alive somewhere. By him being 11 years my mom's senior, it felt like I was running out of time to find him due to the age difference. At one point, this became more of a search for family members on his side, especially siblings. During my search for my father, I never knew that he was on a social media platform. Later I found out that he had videos on YouTube as a world-renowned gospel performer. Who knew?

My baby sister Puddin, my uncle Mane, and me

Chapter 2
The Move

At times, we humans get so involved in a particular phase of our lives that we entirely ignore the other parts. Similarly, when I was in the Air Force, the only thing that mattered to me was my job and my performance. I had no idea what was happening back home or what changes the outside world was going through. My intent in joining the Air Force was to make a career out of it. Unfortunately that didn't pan out due to the situation I was in with my light being threatened. 43 years later I was diagnosed with chronic PTSD in which I still suffer from today. Meanwhile when I got out I rejoined the group that I started with. The prophets of funk and revelation.

Most of the guys in this group were from Sandusky, Ohio, and were mostly siblings . The moment I joined the group, they appointed me as their lead singer, which

I wasn't expecting at all. It was a big change in my life, but I was absolutely loving this change. I would look forward to our jam sessions. Singing was an amazing gift that I later discovered I inherited from my father. I found my voice when I joined our church youth choir . I became one of the lead vocalists in our youth choir. When I was young, I used to sneak out of the window to participate in the elementary school talent shows until my grandmother busted me one night coming through the window. And boy, did not catch it.

I remember my grandmother as a dedicated mother of the church we belonged to. Bethel Apostolic. At this time, no one in my family knew about my musical talents. One Sunday afternoon service, I was given the lead vocals for a song written by our organist, a very grouchy guy but nationally renowned through the Pentecostal Church organization. My grandmother, along with some of her friends, was in the basement of the church preparing after-church dinner. When I struck that first note, I guess someone ran downstairs to the church basement and said sister Cobb, that's your grandson singing. She came running upstairs in her apron, saw me singing, and began to shout all the way down the aisle. That's when she learned about my hidden talents.

After launching my singing career through the church, I started exploring my worldly talents through R&B. After leaving the Prophet's group, I eventually hooked up with a group out of Cleveland they were called The Kinsman Dazz Band. I performed with them locally at a few clubs in Cleveland and eventually left the group to repair some things in my marriage at the time. Later, after things did not work out for me through my marriage, I moved to Atlanta and wound up with a group called The SOS band. I later love that group, also. Now looking back, I wish I had stayed with either one because they both wound up winning Grammy awards. The story of My Life.

I'm going to take a step back for a moment to one of the monumental stages of my life. When I was with the group from Sandusky, I met their sister. This was the first love of my life. Despite her having two small children, we hooked up anyway. Unknowingly my PTSD played a big factor and that not working out. But we did produce an awesome daughter in which it's still a very big part of my life. After splitting up I decided to make my first move to Atlanta to try to repair myself.

Me singing at the Chit Chat lounge
1986 Decatur Georgia.

Chapter 3
The Chitllin' Circuit

After separating from my wife, I struggled with not being able to see our daughter due to a restraining order I kept our home and tried to regroup. I wound up taking on a couple of roommates, my ex-drummer and a pimp-like character named James. My home became chaotic, with lots of women and drugs coming in and out. My home literally became what we call a flop house. During our separation, we started talking about getting back together. With the current situation, I felt the need to relocate to Atlanta to get my family back.

When James and I arrived in Atlanta, his friend was in the process of moving, which was an unexpected surprise. His friend said that if we gave him his deposit, we could move in and take over his apartment, so we did. About two weeks later, we were reported to the rent office and immediately evicted. Our only option was to move across town back in with his friend, who had only two bedrooms and a wife and daughter. So, both James and I slept on the floor and the couch in the living room. On the second day, I met a neighbor upstairs, and she had a spare bedroom, so I moved up there. This did not work out either, as she wanted a relationship, and that was not why I was there. A few weeks later, I was on the streets again.

Once I was homeless again, I met the maintenance man in the apartment complex, and he allowed me to live in an abandoned apartment where I slept in a walk-in closet with all my belongings. James's friend and I found jobs working in construction right outside the complex. After my first paycheck, I was able to obtain an apartment of my own. So began my life in Atlanta alone. This transition actually went pretty well. I put together some equipment and began doing parties at the clubhouse on the apartment grounds. I started making new friends and eventually was able to find a car. Once I could move around Atlanta, I got a better job working for Carolina Freight while DJing in several strip clubs and other venues. My popularity began to grow, and more opportunities became available.

Through James's friend , I met a young lady from Chicago. She was a lovely person, inside and out. Eventually we moved in together. We had a beautiful relationship at first. Later down the line, I found out that she was a lot faster than I was in street life. She and I joined a group of friends from Chicago who were Hebrew Israelites. This was a totally different culture of religion than I grew up in. We became vegetarians, celebrating the Shabbat on Saturdays. The brothers in the house all had multiple spouses. So, eventually, I took on another relationship and moved them in. This turned out to be a disaster. I came home from work one day to find my apartment in disarray. My new friend was gone, and she was still there. So, we moved on from there, left the group, and went back to a normal lifestyle.

We moved in together to the other side of Atlanta, during the time of the Wayne Williams murders. Many missing children were being found in wooded areas throughout our neighborhood. So, we joined the neighborhood group, helping to scour the woods in the area in search of missing children. In October of 1980, I received a letter from my ex-mother-in-law stating that my grandmother had passed. I had been out of touch with my family for over a year. My grandmother was the closest family member to me, so I made preparations to move back to Ohio with my companion. When I returned home, my grandmother had been buried in Alabama along with her deceased sisters in the family churchyard, so I never got to say goodbye to her. Everything was out of whack when I returned. My baby was in a mental ward in the hospital. So, I went and got her and we began cleaning up my grandmother's apartment, which was across the hall from my sister and downstairs for my mother. All three of them lived in the same apartment building. Eventually I hooked up with the local group. We named the group Urban ice. This group had potential. But eventually this group broke up also. But I still knew there was still something missing in my life. My father.

Air Force basic training 1973

My enrollment in the Air Force.

Larry Gibbs bka Doc Heavy, me, DJ Idris.

Me and Urban Ice

Current picture of Skip Martin of the Dazz band and me.

Peabo Bryson and me

Chapter 4
The Restart

Moving forward with my life, I met my little sister's daughter's father , who just got out of the military. Like me, he was Air Force. And he was also the father of my niece, Chrissy. We had a lot in common, especially music. So we decided to combine our equipment, and our music arsenal, and formed a duo, who later became Two Deep Productions. . This name was given to us by one of our fans one night when we were on a roll at this club called to Checkmate . He walked over to us, and said, ya'll are too deep. So we decided to keep the name.

My curiosity about finding my father, although , still loomed large. So I expressed this burning desire to search for my father to my homeboy: So we decide to do this together , but didn't know where to start, so I began asking family members about him again. I did get a little input about his background, so I started calling places in Alabama where he had lived and worked. By me doing this by phone from Ohio, it was hopeless. So I put this back on the back burner till later.

After months of me and my partner McGhee , whom I failed to mention his name earlier, performing together as Two Deep , we decided to change our names. I became DJ Rashaad , and he became DJ Idris. After a good run locally, things started getting rocky with the competition in the streets. The last home club that we played in was called Addis's. This club was wide open, with drugs flowing and the crowd becoming more fierce. But we kept it mellow. After months of gunplay and other bad events, we decided that it was time to make a move. I had decided to return to Atlanta, and he decided to go to Baltimore or DC. After putting our heads together, we both decided to go to Atlanta. We left Canton in a rust bucket of a car with duct tape holding the windshield in place. But we made it with $750 between us. We spent our first night in a motel and then found shelter with some friends we were introduced to. This was like being at home. We lived in a bootleg house and assisted the lady who ran it, Aunt Virginia, the woman who verbally adopted us.

I got a job in downtown Atlanta with a law firm as a courier. This opened a lot of new doors for us. One night, we stopped in a local club in the area where he lived called the Chit Chat Lounge. Their DJ wasn't up to par, so we inquired about an audition. Actually, one night, I came in, and the DJ had slapped a waitress and got fired. So I went to my homeboy's house, grabbed some of his albums, and started playing there. Once they heard me, they hired me, and I brought him in with me. So, the new saga of Too Deep began. After a few months, the club grew in numbers, so they built an add-on to accommodate the crowd. Not only did I DJ, but I also performed with all the live entertainment that came through. Every weekend, we entertained a crowd of around 400 people until 4:00 in the morning. Local record companies brought promos for us to introduce to the public.

During this time, while I was working as a courier, I made plans to travel to Birmingham, Alabama, which was not far away. The law firm I worked for sent me to Birmingham with some docket papers. So Idris and I drove there, took care of business, and began hitting the streets in search of any clearance about my father. We went to the cab company where he used to work, but they no longer had records of him being employed there. We also visited a local funeral home where he had worked, but it was closed.

So we returned to Atlanta, with me being disappointed again about not finding out anything about this man, Johnny Peoples. This made me more determined than ever to continue my search whenever and wherever I could. I had to find out who I was.

After months in Atlanta, I decided to come home and check on my family. I had met someone in Atlanta , and I had become quite fond of her and became engaged. We returned to Canton together. This was a very short-lived engagement because I found out she was very promiscuous, so I sent her back to Atlanta and began my life all over again in Canton, Ohio. During this time, I met my current wife, Doris, for the first time. She lived alone with two children, a boy and a girl. She seemed fragile and alone, in need of someone like me who loved kids and loved her. We dated for several months, but then my PTSD kicked in, and I felt

the need to leave again. So, I packed up and went back
to Atlanta for a third time.

Me, Idris and are adopted family in Atlanta
Home recording studio

Working security at the
St Petersburg Pier Florida.1988

Chapter 5
Reflection

During my third trip to Atlanta, the club I mentioned before, the Chit Chat Lounge, became a job for me that lasted 14 months. During my time there, I took on various roles, including working as a bouncer. In September of 1986, a remarkable moment occurred when I encountered one of the most beautiful creatures I had ever seen. We were both involved in non-committal relationships at the time. Eventually, we met and made the life-altering decision to leave our significant others behind. After only two months of knowing each other, we hastily tied the knot in marriage, marking my second attempt at matrimony.

This second marriage lasted roughly 18 months before she left me and returned to Boynton Beach, Florida. I was left distraught and began drowning my sorrows in heavy drinking. It felt as though a void had returned to my life. I questioned who I was and what my purpose was, especially since I had stopped pursuing my passion for music to embark on this marriage. I was left feeling utterly lost. This response was my initial journey to find closure to find my father or siblings, whichever came first.

Around 1990, I decided to clean up my act up, put my drug addictions and demons behind me, and return to Canton, Ohio, home. I looked up a former girlfriend of mine, Doris who is my current wife . There had been a few additions to her life. She had four beautiful children, which made no difference to me. After a while, we began dating again. After dating for a while, we decided to move in together. In 1994, we decided to have a child together. On March 25, 1995, she gave birth to our lovely daughter, Rashanda Xaneice Cobb. I was 41 years old at the time and began to be a better me. Our daughter had health complications, in which we almost lost her several times. Having our daughter gave us a lifetime bond. On October 16th, 1995, my best friend and his brother-in-law attended the historical Million Man March in Washington, DC. This March was about building relationships with your children, significant others, and family. This opened my mind up to searching for my father again. At this time, technology did not have the tools that eventually led to me finding my father through ancestry DNA.

Around 2020, our eldest daughter did some ancestry research. She discovered that my wife had siblings on her dad's side. My wife was in search of her father and paternal family. Unfortunately, she learned that her father had passed. But, she developed a relationship with her newfound siblings. This prompted me to do a DNA search on ancestry to search for my father or siblings. I had two cousins pop up and contact me. They both combined to eventually find a paternal family in New York. After contacting some cousins in New York, I discovered my dad was still alive at 93 years old, in Brooklyn, right before Father's Day 2021. The irony was that my mom had just passed in January. After making plans for my meeting my dad with his family, I drove to New York on Father's Day and introduced myself to him at our family's church. This was a big surprise to him. Later, I found out that he knew nothing of my existence.

But events prior to finding my father, I reflected for my second failed marriage. They were always children involved in all my relationships, it's drew me closer to find my father. I guess the lack of having my father around drew me into loving all children that didn't have a father. The odd thing about this marriage was that I didn't discover that she had a 15 year old son until 6 months into the marriage. Her child just being raised by his paternal grandparents in Florida. Eventually after 18 months out of the blue, she also left me. In 1988 I moved to St Petersburg Florida with a friend. This adventure became a nightmare and Awakening. Doing my staying in Florida I have been introduced crack cocaine. Exactly three and a half years living in Florida I decided to return home Canton Ohio.

Upon my return home, nothing changed much. My mom was still a gambler and a hustler, and my family was still dysfunctional. My search for identity continued. I decided to check in on a former girlfriend. I found her still living in the same place. She now had four children but was basically single. After dating for a while, we moved in together. This led to us having a daughter together, my third and last daughter. In 1997, we bought a fixer-upper home, in which we still reside today. I eventually became a teacher's assistant with special needs children after several years of taking care of special needs adults. I was forced to retire in 2014 due to an on-the-job injury. It was the beginning of a very hard financial struggle. But God kept his hand on me and my family.

First time having my daughters together my oldest on the left Jackie and my second oldest on the right Chrissy.

Me and Mom on her birthday

Me my mom and my baby sister.

My youngest Rashanda and
my oldest daughter Jackie, who is deceased.

Chapter 6
Confirmation

After learning that my father was still alive, I wasted no time making preparations to go to New York to meet my father for the first time. So the day before Father's Day, My youngest daughter, me, and a friend drove eight hours to Brooklyn, New York, where my father had resided since 1955 when I was only two years old. The excitement of meeting him made the ride seem endless. Upon arrival, we met up with cousin Quatina, who found us hotel accommodations. That morning, we went to the family church where another cousin was the pastor. Everyone knew I was coming, but Dad. I was impatiently awaiting his arrival. I eventually asked who was going to pick him up. They responded; He still drives himself. My jaw dropped. I replied, He still drives at 93 years old? So, we went back to await his arrival.

In January of 2021, another blow to me and my family occurred. My mother, Felounese, passed away in a nursing home due to multiple health issues. After laying her to rest, I resumed my search for closure. In actuality, I was in search of new beginnings. I was connected with another cousin who actually knew my grandmother, Sarah Underwood Peoples. This cousin Anise called me one day and told me to check the obituary of a nursing home in Amityville, New York. This obituary was for one of my first cousins, who had passed. I looked up some of the names in the obituary and began searching for them on Facebook. Two of my second cousins, Quatina and her brother GQ, responded and went to they're elders about me. In June of 2021, I spoke with GQ, and he mentioned an uncle, Johnny. I asked him how old was his uncle. He replied about 90. I was speechless. I said cuz that's my father. This was the Wednesday before Father's Day.

After what seemed to be an eternity, I went to the basement bathroom. When I returned, I was told, your father's here. I replied, don't point him out; I'll spot him. I saw the back of him sitting on the end of a church pue and recognized him immediately. He still fits the description I was told all my. Not to startle him, I returned to my seat with my daughter a few rows ahead of him. I couldn't restrain myself from looking back at him, sitting there with his covid mask on. He was also looking at me with curiosity in his eyes. During the service, I went back to the men's room. When I returned, I decided to sit next to him.

He was sitting alone. We kept looking at one another, so I dropped my COVID mask, pointed to my nose, and told him we had matching bell pepper-shaped noses. I then extended my hand and said, Hello, sir; my name is Robert, and I'm your son.

My dad replied, okay, nice to meet you. To everyone's surprise, we embraced one another. It was unusual for my father to allow a total stranger to hug him. He and I shed tears of joy, and the entire congregation was all crying. When church adjourned, we were surrounded by family and friends. We talked briefly, but I needed to get back on the road to Ohio. I already had his phone number, so I told him we would talk later. The trip home was unbelievable. At last, I had found my biological father after 68 years. I'm still pinching myself today. Yet I still had many questions to ask for him. Did I have siblings, uncles, or aunts?

After returning home, I called him right away. We talked about his past, among other things. I decided to fly back to visit him in New York at my earliest convenience. When I returned, I found he resided alone in a quaint studio apartment. I cooked dinner that evening, and we talked about his life. I found out that he was a renowned gospel singer. His group was made up of mostly family members. They were called Johnny Peoples and the Gospel Crowns. He laughed and said all you had to do was look me up on YouTube. I laughed and said, Dad, who knew? After talking for a while, I found out that he never knew of my existence. But he had no doubt that I was his son. He told me that God told him that something special was about to come his way. And he said it was me.

Chapter 7
A New Beginning

After this visit, I discovered I had three other siblings. Two sisters and a brother. Later, I found that their mother, with whom my dad was still currently married to, had moved to California some 50+ years ago. Dad still does not understand why, but my baby sister Lenora is the only one who stays in touch with him. My sister Lenora and niece Breanna reside in Los Angeles today. We maintain frequent contact. My sister Johnnie Mae passed away some time ago. My brother resides in Las Vegas, along with his family and my sister Johnnie's children. I found out that I was my dad's firstborn. My dad had an amazing life. He left Alabama in 55 to join his baby brother in New York. That's when his music career began.

Upon his arrival in New York, my uncle Willie was already performing with an R&B group. He and my dad were a part of a group called The Brooklyn

Skyways. My dad and his brother, Uncle Willie, eventually joined a group called The Sparks of Rhythm and played several times at the Apollo Theater in Harlem. Dad, like me, became a victim of the streets. Unlike me, Dad never turned to drugs or heavy alcohol use. His addiction was mostly women. According to him, his brothers and father were heavy drinkers when he was growing up. Somewhere along the way, God stepped into my father's life. He left R&B and the streets behind and formed his gospel group. He was gifted with the same ability that was passed on to me. The gift of song and music.

Over the last two years, I have continued to learn more and more about my father. We are covering a lifetime of catching up. Among many of Dad's adventures and accomplishments was his touring on the road with gospel music's finest legends, such as The Mighty Clouds of Joy, The Williams Brothers, and many more. In 2002, while on a gospel tour, my dad was the recipient of the key to the city of his hometown of Birmingham, Alabama. My dad is still performing. I've met several of his band members. In March of 2023, my dad invited me to a gospel concert in New York. I had been out of touch with gospel music for a long time. Little did I know my dad was to be the main attraction. Towards the end of the program, Dad and I began walking towards the stage. The audience started standing and applauding. Dad and I walked on stage, and he was honored as the last man standing from his era of gospel music.

That was an amazing event. After Dad spoke of his gratitude and appreciation towards his ongoing fans, most had assumed he had passed, like most all of his predecessors. I was so proud I had to speak on his behalf. I first reassured the audience that it wasn't his bodyguard but that I was his long-lost son. I told them that God is capable of doing anything. I gave them a brief part of my journey to find this man, my father, John Edward Peoples, and the 68 years to find him. The audience began to weep and applaud our testimony. As we left the stage, walking up the aisle, people were reaching over one another just to touch my father. This was so surprising to him that he had been so remembered and loved. And to have his oldest son by his side.

Since meeting my dad, he constantly reminds me of how empty his world was before The Most High brought us together. His words are, I was just like a ball rolling around and knowing which away he was gonna roll next. But my favorite quote is the best is yet to come. And the best is still coming. He also told me that my grandmother, Sarah Underwood, was an amazing woman and mother and a devoted child of God. I have pictures of her, and I regret not being able to hold her and hang on to her apron strings. Even though my grandfather, John Wesley Peoples, was a piece of work that God chose to take very early, I wish I had known him too. To both of you, I love and miss you from the bottom of my heart 💗, and I look forward to seeing you someday.

During our rides back and forth to New York, we listened to a large variety of music, from jazz to gospel music. I loved to sing along, and that is how Dad got exposed to my voice, which is still very good, I think. He loves my voice, so our next goal is to do a recording together. I have access to all his musical tracks, so I'm rehearsing his music. The purpose of my writing this book is to briefly tell my story of how persistence, faith in the highest, and the termination of never giving up can make anything come true. I hope and pray that sharing this short but precious story will be encouraging to any and everyone who has faced these types of circumstances. May God bless and keep everyone who reads my story to always continue to trust in God. The beginning!!

Chapter 8
Pictorial

One of dad's first Gospel albums

Dad's first R&B group

*Dad receiving the key to the
city of Birmingham Alabama*

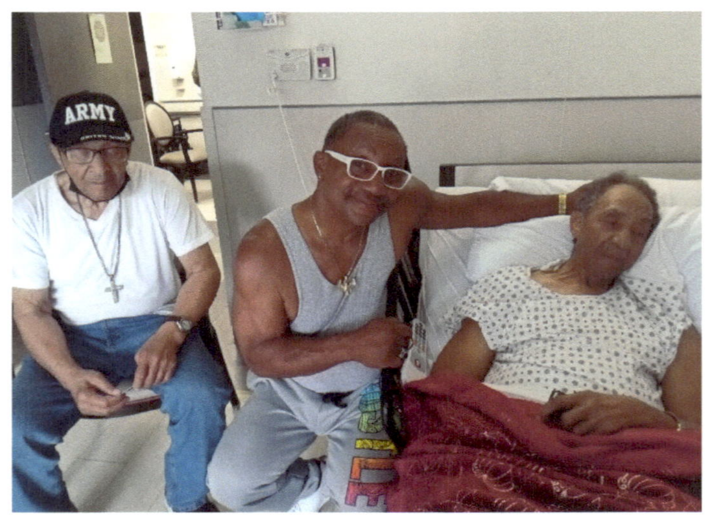

Me Dad and Uncle Willie

Me and Dad hanging out

Me and Dad in Brooklyn

Me and Dad united for ever

My Mother

My Father

My deceased sister Johnnie Mae bka Freda

My deceased uncle Leslie

My baby sister and mom

Robert Cobb, 68, of Canton, shows a photo of himself and his long-lost father, John Peoples. Cobb used a DNA website to locate Peoples, who didn't know Cobb existed. They met each other for the first time on Father's Day last year. CHARITA M. GOSHAY/CANTON REPOSITORY

Canton man finally finds long-lost dad after 68 years

Charita M. Goshay Canton Repository | USA TODAY NETWORK

CANTON – Sometimes it takes time to get an answer to a prayer. ● For Canton resident Robert Cobb, it took a lifetime — 68 years to be exact. ● Cobb was born in Birmingham, Alabama, in 1953 to a teenage mother and a 25-year-old man who left the area without learning about the pregnancy. Cobb and his father John "Johnny" Peoples, a renowned gospel singer who lives in Brooklyn, New York, wouldn't meet until last year on Father's Day.

See FATHER, Page 8A

The Canton Repository article about me and Dad.

Dad receiving a gospel music achievement recognition

My dad's gospel group, featuring my cousins.

The Gospel Crowns

www.ingramcontent.com/pod-product-compliance
Lightning Source LLC
Chambersburg PA
CBHW040855110726
48005CB00001B/78